Chasing Myself

By Caroline White
-cwpoet

Almost five years ago, without warning, I lost my father to a sudden heart attack. It was a difficult time in my life when I was so focused on structure and control and
eventually lost both.
His death was extremely difficult for me to accept and I am still handling this loss on a day-to-day basis. It led me down a very scary path of depression and anxiety. It also caused tramatic issues in my marriage and my social life.
I use running and writing to combat it.

For you, Dad.

Love,
Caroline

Pacing

My favorite running partner runs in heaven now.

This Life

This life twists
and it turns us,
it lifts and it burns us
never giving us a break
always reminding us
of what we cannot take
we've started to believe
that there are rules
and that's what makes
all of us fools.
There are no rules
you need to face
life is all just one
big race.

Run

I would run to the ends
of the earth and back
if it meant I could escape her.
She fuels my anger,
ignites my drive,
and pushes me harder
not to be her any longer.

She hasn't done anything wrong,
in fact I'm sure she's grown quite strong,
I am just done.

With her,
and this chapter.

Chasing Myself

I am
constantly
chasing myself,
to leave
the dead
behind.

I cried
as I kissed
myself
goodbye.
I was too young,
but ready,
to die.

Depression

Some people think that depression
is all about being sad.
It isn't.
My defense mechanism
happens to be laughter,
so you would never know that
I lack a sense of self-value.
There are two things
that make me feel
like myself again:
-when someone notices something
  that makes me feel good about myself and
-the absence of unnecessary criticism.
It's not difficult to make someone feel valued.
Do it.

Good Day

Sleepy-eyed and in love,
drinking coffee in bed
dancing in public,
singing outside of my head.
Dressed to the nines
with gigantic smiles,
fresh-baked blueberry pie,
and running for miles.
Sure of myself
and all that I say,
open to the world
in every possible way.
This is the me
that I laugh at
on a good day.

Bad Day

Shaken with doubt,
covers over my head
lights off
curtains drawn
I'm not leaving this bed.
Tight-lipped,
dressed in blankets
with no appetite.
Running until it hurts
deep into the night.
Crying in the shower
trapped in hell – JUST GO AWAY!!!
I am everything I hate
on a bad day.

Chasing Myself

Wind

With skin
so thin
I fear
the wind
so cold
so strong
so right
so wrong
it burns
it stings
it tears
my wings.
This wind
please end,
let me soar
again.

Parts of me

There are parts
that live in me
only to destroy me.
I can't understand why.
And if they don't destroy me,
they find a way to someone I love.
I can't stand this about me.
I don't understand why
I tip-toe over happiness
just to run to pain.
Even when I know
that the things I chase
will hurt me the most,
I want them more,
because I am a part of them.

Undertow

It's not the undertow
that frightens me anymore,
it's the failure to recognize the sun
once my body
is washed
back ashore.

Worry

Some people worry about me,
not the ones who really know me
just the ones who think they do.
The ones who don't know what
I've been through,
the ones who haven't stuck around long
they'll never know this kind of "strong".

Missing

I am
missing
myself.
I am lost
I am tired
I am busy
I am wired.
I am the 4 am version of a party
that has overslept,
I am the queen on the side of a mirror
that doesn't reflect.
I am laughter
that has turned into tears
and nobody has even
looked for me
in years.

September Moon (Laura)

Sipping wine
under the September moon,
I look over at your tears
and I cannot stop them.
They stream down a face
that has blinked,
smelled,
and tasted so much pain.
You are completely broken
and I can't fix you,
you are bitter and mad at God
and I don't blame you.
I know better than to give you advice
so I wipe your tears,
one by one
and pray that tomorrow
you see the sun.

Silence

Silence on the outside
is what killed us,
Silence on the inside
is what killed me.

We stopped listening
we stopped talking
but I still heard you.
Nothing is louder than silence.
Actually, the only thing
louder than silence
is the inevitable breakdown
that it eventually births.
Years of silence
will fucking take you down
in a matter of seconds.
It comes out uglier
than the silence, itself.
It stains the people it touches.
Stains turn into scars
and scars will always remind me
of silence
and how I died.

Cover

Cover me with your sorrow
blanket me with tomorrow,
steady me, ease this pain,
whisper softly, love, again.
Touch this skin
so light, so soft.
Do not stop
until I am lost.
Away from people
is where I stay
and try to
dream another day.
I need your closeness
more than ever,
cover me now,
until forever.

Slip

Walking on the edge
was never enough,
so she danced
and she slipped
just to prove
she was tough.

Light

Somedays
the light at the end of the tunnel
is just too bright
and staying wrapped
inside of darkness
feels cozy, warm, and tight.

Rhythm

My feet hit the ground
a rhythm is created,
stride after stride
I bring out the things I hide.

-why did you do that? Shame!
-why did I let you? Pain!
-how do I get out? Change!

And I run.

I run until my body goes
from strong to weak
waiting for the rush,
the surge, the release.
I'm fixing this girl
one mile at a time.

I do not run for the thrill of it
I run,
for the kill of it.

Dead

Dead, she just lies there.
I couldn't have done anything to help her,
I was scared to death of her.
The horror that befell her was evident
on her face, on her skin, in her eyes.
The words that bled from her heart
were those of complete misery
smashed down her throat
with brutal force.
She didn't belong here anymore
but she couldn't do anything about it,
she wouldn't even try.

So I slipped back into her skin
and pulled her up
and we ran away together.

She's in a better place now
and if anyone threatens her
they'll have to go through me.

He wasn't worth losing her
but she'll never see him again.

Crash

If the earth were
ever to apologize
for how brutally
I crashed into it,
it would continue
to bring me butterflies
to remind me
you're still in it.
Your spirit flies,
on delicate wings,
in sunsets,
in rain,
and when
the wind sings.

Darkness

I beg her to let go
of the dark. The darkness
that lives inside of her.
She has yet to listen.
It is not the darkness
that she fears.
For in the blackest black
of the dark she is hidden.
After this long it's all she
knows, grasps, and breathes.
You can offer her the light,
but it tastes of metal,
it feels of fire,
it sounds of screeching pain,
and it smells of rotting flesh.
Leave her be.
This sensory overload is not
worth such madness.
She just fucking prefers the dark.
Give it to her.

Now go.

Tripping

Today, as I was running
through my head,
I tripped over a thought
and cut my knee on this idea...
what if all this time
I was getting better,
I was really getting worse?
And all of the lies
you spoon-fed me
were to shut me up
so that nobody would know
that you took advantage of me
when I was at my lowest.
Building me up, erasing my frown
maybe you are the sick one,
with another pill,
I'll wash that down.

Duty, Honor, Country

The thundering jolt
of an unexpected gun salute
forced me out of my skin.
The sheer terror of
already broken and shaking,
compounded with blood-curdling,
remorseless noise…
felt like stepping off of a chair
under a barbed wire noose.

There is no recovery.
There is no forgetting.

Duty.
Honor.
Country.

You were honored well,
but the sound
I was unprepared for
still electrocutes me.
Nightly.

Coma

I felt particularly displaced
when I got the call that you were in a coma.
They said they'd know more in an hour
and that hour lasted a lifetime.
It lasted long enough for me to feel you
leaving this world,
but not long enough
for me to convince God
that I still needed you here.
I figured he would at least let me get to you
since none of us had any warning.
But he didn't.
I don't remember much of the plane ride
but I do remember holding
your dead hand.
I thought that all you needed
was my hand in yours,
to come back to life.
That was very foolish of me.

Caroline

Caroline is the name
of a girl who is happy.
Caroline laughs all the time,
until she cries.
Caroline smiles at everyone she sees,
while she looks them in their eyes.
Caroline is beautiful and confident
and as poised, as poised can be.
I'm just not convinced anymore,
that Caroline is me.

Chasing Myself

Perfection

Her propensity for perfection
is powerful, peculiar, and poetic.
Properly placed pretty packages
pleasantly positioned, just so.
Perfectly proportional paper-thin
physique primed and polished.
Privately and procedurally she paces
in a painfully painted prison of purgatory,
pleading for permanent paradise.

Requiem

I choreographed a dance
to my requiem.
I remembered how light you made me feel,
so I incorporated slow and subtle movements.
I remembered how boldly you reached for my body
so I incorporated thunderous and exaggerated movements.
And then I remembered how hideously you
broke my heart.
So I ran as fast as I could to escape the pain,
but I died.

Dancing to my own funeral.

I forgive you

I forgive you
for isolating and abandoning me.
I forgive you
for clinging tightly to your silence
while I became best friends
with vodka and violence.
I forgive you
for walking away and keeping me in limbo,
begging you to stay
I forgive you
because its time…to push through.

I need to find a way to forgive myself,
for losing me
to you.

Dancer

The darkness creeps in
with the greatest of ease,
as majestic as an ocean breeze.
It permeates the air
until it's all that I can breathe
and it takes me down
to my withering knees.
I never know
when it plans to leave.

Depression is a slow dancer
that always has the lead.

Synthetic Guilt

It's no surprise that you can only go so long,

submerged in your own misery

before you leap out of hell

to explore new horizons,

new feelings, and new people.

You'll try them on to see how they fit.

Oddly enough,

they don't have to be the right size to be wanted,

they just have to mirror your wants and desires in some

similarly comfortable way

that you understand.

You'll feel guilt,

but this guilt is somewhat synthetic.

You've taught yourself to feel this guilt

just for the simple fact that

living in misery teaches you

to find the worst in yourself.

Sweet Dreams

I sleep wonderfully
every night
thanks to pills…
I still wake up
reaching
for your ghost.
I still wake up hoping
it was all a nightmare.
It wasn't.
So I will remind myself again,
tomorrow,
and the next day,
and the next day.

Reflection

I prayed for all hell
to break loose
and somehow you appeared.
Your hands looked jealous
of my neck,
your eyes sharply
locked onto mine
while you hungrily glared
at my pain.
You ate it up,
you soaked it all in,
and withheld all comfort,
when you should've loved me the most.

Never again
has my reflection
encountered that hideous ghost.

Time

We frivolously
dance around in time,
as if we have
all of it
in the world
to spare.

A suffocating reality
makes the truth
so hard to bear.

Time is not a healer.
Time is but a joke.
Time is running
away from me
as fast as you
and your ghost.

Policy

I have seen honesty…
and how smooth
of a breeze it offers.
I have also seen it
become a tornado
with its trajectory unplanned
and its victims indiscriminant.
A path of total torment
and irreparable destruction.
I have my own policy.

It's probably different from yours.

Faithful

I don't want it
but please don't take it away.
It toys with me often,
it leaves unannounced
just to remind me who's boss.
But it always comes back,
fast enough to ever notice it left.
You can find me in my bed
or in a heap, on the floor
of my shower.
It will push me to the
highest of hills,
into the blackest of nights,
all the while knowing
I am terrified of heights.
Just to flirt with its edge.
When it's faithful
I am safe, I am numb.
Depression, you are mine.
You might be the most faithful thing
I have ever known.

Dopamine (Mom)

I feel sorry for her,
it isn't her fault
that she trembles and tremors,
it takes a stab at my heart.
Her disease will be vile
it will imprison her,
to a body void of balance
when all I've ever seen from her is grace.
It's sad how life can be so mean
but it's worse in her world.

Without dopamine.

Wrong way

I never liked the taste of liquor
but I loved where it took me
and how fast it got me there.

Until the time I got lost
and couldn't find my way back.

Broken walls,
broken pictures,
broken hearts.

I will never lose me again.

Don't tell me to fucking smile, thanks

I drop my kid off at dance class
and I go see a therapist.
I run until my legs burn.
I cry, sometimes, for no reason at all,

You might judge me for this,
but I don't give a shit.
I didn't ask for depression.
It came after me,
It took all that it wanted from me,
right after my dad died.
Damn near took my marriage with it.

Don't feel sorry for me.
Just don't tell me to fucking smile
if I'm not already doing so.

Rain

Every lonely day
I wish for you
in my bed, to lay
face to face
like back in the day,
hanging onto words
each of us would say.
Laughing too loudly at jokes
and faces,
never even knowing
that there would be traces
of love leaking slowly,
like air from a tire
while resentment and guilt
replaced our big fire.
Our hearts are scarred now
with layers of pain
and that's what makes me want
more rain.

Grey

She sits
silently still
absorbing all of the grey,
all of the dark,
and all of the rain.
This alone,
will make the sun
shine brighter
upon its inevitable return.

Bottled up

Tears rained
down her cheeks
as she held back
more than anyone
could bear.
She kept rage bottled up
in there.
She knew
it was better
to get it out
but she just didn't dare.
Until the day
her world exploded,
leaving her nothing,
in thin air.

The truth about time

We say:
"time heals all wounds"
because it would be rude
to say nothing at all.
Even worse;
to say the truth:
"death stops time".

Run

It's time
for me to run.
To escape
this stagnant hope,
before I trip into a world
that's filled with hanging rope.
I've always held you dear to me
and this I must confess,
I couldn't love you more…
and never any less.

I'm sorry

She trusted me and I let her down.
Not as much as she usually did
but it's cruel to compare secrets,
weaknesses, and even breaking points
for that matter.
But I led her down the path
of another break to her heart
after I promised I wouldn't.
I wouldn't let this vulnerable part of me
be broken again.
Part of her is pissed
and I'm actually afraid
to see what she will do.
So all I did tonight, was go for a run,
while I repeatedly told myself
"I'm sorry"…

I cried and accepted my own apology.

For no reason

My problem
is the rush I feel
to my chest
-for no reason.
Just a swarm of
invisible butterflies
that turn into wasps
in my stomach.
I shake,
because I'm nervous
-for no reason.
The thoughts
slither in and I have
no choice but to
gasp for air
-for no reason.
And sometimes
anxiety just hangs on
and on, and on
-for no reason.

Chasing Myself

Death the deceiver

Death
doesn't borrow memories
it doesn't take them either.
Death records over memories
so that all of the good
become bad,
all of the happy ones, sad.
Death laughs at you,
it pokes, it prods
it pushes you down
cement staircases
that have no end.
It distorts faces,
it makes others laugh
the laugh of the one who's gone.
Death visits you while
you are sleeping
just to haunt you in a dream.
And of all things…
why does death want my
sleep so badly?

A sea

She casts her heart out
to a dark and dangerous sea
she reels and reels with pain,
nothing returns
but the line.
This will better suit her, now.
Feelings are too messy,
they always need to be explained.

And what is the point
when nobody can hear her?

Heavy

I could never drink
just to remember you.
In fact, I don't so I won't.
It's not that I don't miss you
I just don't take the risk.
A few drinks and a few songs later
and I'm flooded with pain.
And the tears.
They never end,
until I wake up the next day
with my head feeling heavy,
and my eyes swollen with liquid memories
that I tried not to lose.
My heart broken, yet again,
but somehow lighter.
More of you escaped me.
People look at me like I have a fucking problem.
Well I do, I don't want to let you go.
They say I should let it all out,
but pain is all I have left, of you.
I can't lose that.
I won't.

The style of a broken heart

They always tell me I look good
when I am sad.
I've always worn
a broken heart well.
I am most put together
when I am holding it all in.

It's my style.

Cursive

She speaks in perfect cursive,
dancing around all of the lies
and the truth.
Dotting all of the pain
with fake smiles and hearts.
She speaks in perfect cursive,
painting breathtaking pictures
of the most beautiful denial.

Chasing Myself

OCD

That which did not kill me
did not make me stronger.
It made me a different person.
A weaker, scared, ever so
constantly ruminating over
every impossible
and inappropriate thing
that couldn't and wouldn't ever happen, person.
Not again anyway.
Losing someone you love
will never make you stronger.
It makes your time on earth
feel longer.
It makes you look over your shoulder more,
it makes looks of disgust, at the mirror,
feel like forever.
It makes peace within, seem like never.
It makes alcohol a weapon,
it makes love a lesson.
It makes smiles seem unreal,
it makes the time I hate me
stand still.

Tighter

Pain
is my
security
blanket
The tighter I
am wrapped,
the better.

Hell

Some problems
are so
deep-rooted,
we'd have to
go to hell
to fix them.

Darkness

Darkness
wonderfully
welcomes me home.
Inside of this darkness
I am never alone.
I wish for you,
inside this pain,
but gladly
from darkness,
I keep secret,
your name.

Wave

There is a wave
that slowly approaches
it tickles my toes,
then it recedes.
The next time back,
it's up to my knees.
It usually flirts with
my thighs and my hips,
but some days it rises
way past my lips.
I struggle,
I choke,
I eventually lose.
I am melancholy and quiet,
undertaken with blues.
It is a peaceful demise
with its tender embrace,
it kisses my neck
and caresses my face.
Before I know it
I am washed back ashore
and ready for the next day's excursion,
once more.

Chasing Myself

Be weak

Don't speak.
Be weak.

Be paralyzed under the trees,
still shaking at the knees.
There's nobody who will save you
there's nobody else that craves you.
You're alone now.
In the dark now.
And you will stop breathing
and start seething
and fucking run
from the gun
that wakes you up at night
and makes you lose your fight.

Be weak.
Don't speak.

It is less of a fight,
this way.

Sadness

You would think sadness hurts
but sometimes it doesn't
because I cannot feel
these tears that roll down my cheeks.
I cannot feel this heart that beats,
or these lungs that breathe.
All I feel is empty,
and emptiness
is the loneliest feeling before
you go numb.
Emptiness plays with my mind.
It tells me I am not worth
the breaths that are breathed,
the blood that is pumped,
or these tears that I've cried
Emptiness yells at me to shut up.
So I do.

Pain

She's seen
so much pain.
Pain is who she is.
Pain is her idol.
Pain is her comfort.
Pain is her lover.
Pain is her friend.
Pain is her answer.
Pain is her hobby.
Pain is her job.
Painfully, I get it.

Colder

It's colder today
the weather, not my heart.
The smell of stagnant essence
creepily blows through the air.
The wind is sharp but helpful,
it reminds me to keep moving,
Although I do wish to be back
in my cradle of blankets and safety.
People are dressed in layers
of clothes and sadness.
Their faces remind me to keep moving,
to keep seeking warmth
but not at a cost,
not independent of you.
It's colder today,
the world, but not my heart.

Running

Running was always a choice
I thought I was making
until my father died.
I grabbed every single feeling
swallowed it deep inside,
and ran.
Without ever knowing what I was running from.
I thought I was running from pain
but pain was always running at the same pace as me.
I thought I was running from reality
but I soon lost any understanding of reality
to even recognize anything outside of
vodka and doom.
I did run from communication
which cut off any outward ties I had with anyone and everyone
who could help me.
When I thought I was asking for help,
I realized I was running from help
because accepting help
meant accepting the problem.
And I,
was just fine in my brokenness...
until I realized
it was running,
that broke me.

Chasing

You can't untangle my wild.

I am

I am lost
I am found
I am six feet underground.
I am high,
In the sky
I am happy
but I cry.
I am love
I am hate
I am early
I am late.
I am me
take me or don't,
but break your heart
I promise,
I won't.

Hell is where I left her

I was pushed
down that spiral,
landing in burning flames.
Fighting and screaming
for someone to stop all the blame.
At the bottom,
I died,
I left that part of me behind
and with bruises and wounds,
from that hell,
did I climb.
Some say that I'm better,
but I'll never know,
because I don't remember
the girl
I let go.

Goodbyes

I hate goodbyes.
The last breath drawn from inside
a sold, childhood home.

The smell of Grandma's house,
long before she is laid to rest
and a new family moves in.

The tightness of a hug
before a divorce is final.

I take thise goodbyes and I keep them,
even though I'd kill not to.
I tell myself, as I walk away,
"this is the last time".
I walk down this driveway,
I smell this home-cooking,
I feel this heart beat against mine.
Then my heart familiarly shakes
and then sinks,
while I take a permanent picture
of goodbye, with my eyes.

Bridge

I ran today
over the bridge
of troubled waters.
They still flow
unapologetically
while all of the pain
in my body
begs me not to.
I run to you
for strength,
for comfort,
for love,
and those waters roar.
I will never tame them
so I run faster
each time.

Trying not to hear them scream
that you were never mine.

Skin

I mischievously shed my skin
I climbed out of it and ran
from dark clouds that incessantly
tried to strike me,
from words that interminably
tried to bite me.
Into your arms
that encircled me
so tightly.
You've disappeared now.
I can't find my skin
and even if I could
it wouldn't fit, any longer.

Giving up

While I should be
chasing sleep
my mind drifts
elsewhere,
to a place where you doze
wrapped in blankets,
that I have never felt.
Wrapped in arms,
that are not mine.
Wrapped in love,
that is not true.
I would guess
that you miss me too.
But giving up
is what I will do.

Grave

He sleeps
in a cold grave
blanketed by resentment.
Constantly dreaming
of freedom,
never escaping his nightmare.
Sometimes he takes
my dignity with him.
He is a fool to think
that dragging me down
will make him stronger.

I was born to run.

Edge

I dance on a thin and rusty edge
of hating and loving you.
I'd pick one direction
or the other
but it's too exhausting,
since I do both.
I hate you.
But if I ever fell
I'd still want your love
to rescue me.
If you didn't,
I'd never forgive you.

Not that I had planned on it anyway.

Circles

Circles.
I remember circles.
Spinning.
I definitely remember
the spinning.
And even after my body stopped
the insides of my head
kept at it.
Boy, was it busy and turbulent.
And the only person I saw who could help
was you.
But you didn't.
And although we locked eyes
you never stopped me.

From spinning.

Mess

I will admit I'm a mess,
everything I do,
everything I love
falls apart
at some point in time.
But my second chances
are always worth it.
I will always be a mess…
a tornado, a clown, a bitch, a lover,
a friend, a time-bomb, a baby, a mother.
I promise if I destroy you,
I'll put you back together.

Maybe and probably
a little bit better.

Rain

I like running
in the rain.
Nobody can see your tears
or tell how sad you are.

Goodbye

As the sun
divorces the sky
and the moon rivals
the diamonds on high,
I lay in my casket and cry
the tears of an unjust goodbye.

Caroline White

Lines

You left me
at my worst,
that's how I know
my second chance
is my last chance.
I walked these lines
to get you back,
and now
I'm doing so good,
I'm running them.
These lines keep me
from losing control.
As long as I stay on them
this last chance
will last.

Chasing Myself

Somewhere

Somewhere between
now and forever
a giggle is floating
as light as a feather.
A whispered goodbye,
I haven't caught yet
though I search and I search
with a lantern and net.
I left her outside,
said I'd be back real soon.

And now she is lost
between here and the moon.

Mirror

I can open my eyes
as wide as can be
in front of a mirror
it just isn't me.
But hazel against blue,
when my mirror is you,
I feel whole
I see you
in my soul.

Chasing Myself

Laura

It was always like us
to lose track of time.

Remember when 1 turned into 12
and the red wine didn't even spill?
All of the songs we cried to
while telling each other it was going to be okay?
I believed that.
I really believed that.

Now all I wish for,
is that time would just lose track
of us.

Faith, hope, and love

I just can't apologize
for loving people
the way I do.
Even the ones I shouldn't love.
It's the only side
of me that's soft.
It's who I am
it's how I measure myself
it's how I measure you,
I wasn't wired to love
on faith and hope alone.

Armor

Take all the armor off,
be vulnerable,
learn who you are,
and then fall
so messily and mercilessly in love
that the only person who recognizes you
is you.

And the person you take down
with you.

Love is a drug

There's nothing worse than the
false hope that love gives,
when love tells you
"anything is possible",
it robs you of reason.
Love makes you do impossible things,
it makes you believe impossible people.
It tricks you into taking risks.
Love manipulates you into thinking
"you'll never know unless you try",
that's where it gets you.
Love is a drug.
An addictive, abusive,
asshole of a drug.
If you've never known this then you've just
kept your hands clean of the bloodiest of hearts.
Good for you,
you win.
Or do you?

Love is a drug.
And I am 2 days clean.

Gone

When I wasn't ready
love grabbed me off of the ground
and ran with me.

Pulling me through the dark,
pulling me through branches,
pulling all of the air from my lungs.

Then love let go.
I chased after it
faster than I'd ever ran before
but it was still faster than me.
I hid behind a corner and waited
but love never came back.

I'm ready now,
and love is gone.

Born

I was born in no hurry
on a cold December night,
with pale skin and green eyes
that sparkle in the light.
A smile that has always
been quite contagious,
a temper that some have seen,
so outrageous.
A laugh that's so loud
and never unknown,
but the stare and the glare
that can turn hearts to stone.
I like to make others happy
I believe I always will,
but beware of my dark side
the biggest part of me, still.

Game

He dresses up,
just to corrupt my mind.
Love to him,
is but a game.

He is darkness
he helps pull me under,
without a care
as to whether I
will land on my feet or not.
He is fickle,
only wanting
what he wants
when he wants it,
always with the intent
to destroy me.
And once I let him,
he shows back up,
as handsome as ever
to rescue me.
He is the one.
Who won't let go.

Drawn

I am drawn to the diamonds
in the black sea above,
I am drawn to the weakness in those
who can't find self-love.
I am drawn to lovely,
quiet, empty spaces.
I am drawn to frowns
and distance in faces.
I am drawn to laughter
and how it's contagious.
I am drawn to noise
and all things outrageous.
I am drawn to wild
and crazy, and free.
I am drawn to you
and you are drawn to me.

Mistake

You lie
I break
I cry
you take
you try
I shake
bye-bye
mistake.

Sober

With as intoxicating
as love is,
it's not a bad thing
to be sober.

Blueprints

I asked you for the blueprints
to your mind,
so I could casually dance inside
once more.
Instead, you gave me
the blueprints to your heart
and forgot to draw one single door.

Give me

Give me
the freedom
to stand on my own,
the trust
to search for myself,
and your arms
for when I mess
it all up.

Racing

Lets run all the way…away. Together.

Down

My mirror
introduces me
to the sickness
in my eyes.
There is no such
idea of a smile today.
Please excuse
my absence
from your game,
I cannot pretend
to be okay.

Secrets

My best kept secrets
are owned
by the moon.

Hanging above
all the other's heads,
while sound asleep
in innocent beds.
The moon glows
knowingly,
at me, not scared.
For it's my soul
that's been
opened, stripped, and bared.

Wild

You couldn't handle my wild.

It's not a challange.
It's just an observation.
Depression loves me,
half of the time, in bed
the other half running,
climbing, obsesssing over the moon.
That moon though.
It rules everything, pretty much.
I feel sorry for those with depression,
but more for those
who do not struggle with it
It doesn't make a whole lot of sense.
But that doesn't mean
that you can tell me to "smile",
or "this too shall pass".
Yeah, you can shove those words
up your ass.
Just don't say them. Just listen.
Listen with you ears,
listen with your eyes,
listen with your heart.

I wont break.

But listen, watch, feel.

Call me if you haven't heard from me,

Approach me if I look sad

just fucking notice me.

When I'm having a bad day

don't sweep me under the rug.

Pushing me away makes it worse.

It makes me float

farther from this earth.

But if you pretend not to notice,

you aren't helping me,

you are just helping yourself.

Sorry

With the moonlight
spilling down your face,
I told you I was sorry.
I practiced those words
all day.
You were tight-lipped
the whole time
and walked away.
With my blood and tears
boiling and flowing,
I realized that
you should've been sorry.
And with no more
tears left to cry
and no words left to say,
I am sure that you will
practice what
you should've said.
For the rest of your life.

Chasing Myself

Steady

Pain
changed her
into someone
she had no choice but to love.
Hurt that turned into anger,
that turned into drive.
Atop her pedestal,
she could see her faults dancing beneath her,
hand-picking the ones she would save.
Crushing the ones she wouldn't,
under a strong and steady foot.

Remember

The sun dances seductively
through the curtain
I forgot to close.
It's telling me to rise,
get up, and get out of bed.
The rain is over.
I will.
I will get up,
drink some coffee
and think about happiness. Again.
I might open all of the curtains today.
I might practice smiling
at my reflection.
I do have a lot to be happy about.
That's what I need to remember.

Chasing Myself

Cartwheel

I heard you
in someone's laugh today
and I giggled out loud.
The way I hijack
these moments,
would make you so proud.
Maybe in our next lives
we will be
connected in space
and time.
Like always,
you looking for me,
either two steps ahead
or a cartwheel behind.

More

I am alive today, because I feel more-
more than I usually allow myself to feel.
It's hard to feel more,
it's tiring, but I have to keep going they say.
They say it will get easier.
Easier to do what? Forget?
Forget how hard it was to let you go?
How should I become desensitized to the
fact that earth has swallowed you whole?
How do I let, just let, you sleep in the ground? Forever.
And the thought of all of this makes me feel less.

This fast, I feel less.
And I remind myself
that less is more.

Chasing Myself

Again

I lay here in the dark
and breathe.
I think of the things I wish to have said,
I think of how much time had passed
since you shared this earth with me
I think of all of the times I still
reach for the phone to call you,
laugh about something you told me,
see your smile on my son's adorable face,
your will of steel in my daughter's demeanor.
Should have done more,
said more,
loved more.
I know that you are here. I see you.
I know that you are close. I feel you.
I know I need to let you go. To heal me.
I know that you will always love me
and I cannot wait to see you again.

Sun

She knew
she could get
through each
night with the
sun on the
other side of it.

She knew
she could freeze
in the darkness
and melt in
the basking glow of
the biggest star.

Dance

All around her
is music and laughter
and she dances
to the beat of
happily ever after.
She's beautiful
and brave,
so graceful and light.
She twinkles like
a star,
in the darkest
of nights.

Silver linings

She softly spoke of
of seasons passed
seducing the ears of
someone who asked.
Smiling slyly,
she stops to remember
soft lips and shaking hands
in a secret September.
Slowly savoring
the size of her sins,
with sparing remorse
she searches within.
Steadily and slowly
she swallows her pain
and spies silver linings,
to shine after rain.

Easier

I need to be easier on myself,
that's what he always told me.
And maybe, for once, I could
let him drive me today.
Just to see where the wind takes us,
just to remember my tiny hand in his,
just to remember his after-shave
and how it smelled of Christmas and home.
Just to remember the Eagles playing on the stereo,
just to remember how close we still are.

Even though he lives in heaven now.

Caroline White

Paths

I walked
these paths alone
without the people I needed.
I get offended
when people say
I'm strong for that.
That makes it sound
like I was ever given a choice.

Forbidden

She dances effortlessly
with a furious amount if grace,
in and out and all around
the most forbidden
corners of life.

Chasing Myself

Naked Trees

I love looking outside
to see fall leaves,
flying through a bright blue sky.
The trees are undressing themselves
and while their clothing is incredibly stunning,
with such embellished hues.
I like the thin and jagged
frames of the trees,
they remind me of
BALLERINAS AND SKELETONS!
I especially love them against a white, frosted background.
I love fall, the shedding of trees,
and the dancing naked trees.

Karma

Like a Cheshire cat
she smiled as she sat
rememebering all of his dreams.
He promised her love
yet he rose aboove
and laughed at the pain
in her screams.
He still hasn't found
a woman to crown,
he pretends he is happy alone.
I'm sad for him, really
because life is so silly,
Karma's the biggest bitch
I have known.

Strings

The strings that suspend me from heaven
are just strong enough to keep me from hell,
I am just a tease to the earth below me
the ground would swallow me whole if I fell.

Dance Again

And sometimes
when
nobody
is looking,
she steps
out of her skin
and begins
to dance
again.

Same Track

There is a shift at mile 2
as caffeine takes over my stride
my mind races to heaven,
to be eased and to run by his side.
Miles 3 and 4 fly by me
I won't look at my time,
or my pace.
It's only me and him out here
pushing through,
with strength and grace.
Mile 5, oh how I have missed you Dad
for just one day - to have you back,
but I know that I'll see you tomorrow,
same time
same pace
same track.

Heal

It will hurt more to heal
than to just stay in the pain
you'll have to embrace it
and then,
one day-
you'll realize you're stronger
and it hurts less
and your smile is back
and you're you
again.

Soft

There's a soft understanding
in my heart today,
replacing a toxic and anxious maze.
Tranquility wisps through every breeze,
I see sunlight
where I rest my gaze.
I hope this feeling will last
but I won't count on it,
just in case.
For now I will savor each moment
of feeling this weightless,
in space.

Scars

The scar tissue
constricting
my heart
is a constant
reminder of why
we forgive
but never forget.
We continue to live
with needs
that go unmet
while searching
for a life
that we won't regret.
Yet, still hold on
tighter
to something not meant,
all the while
without breaking
a sweat...
and we call that "love".

Empty

I hear the emptinesss
I feel today.
It sounds of a lulling piano
and a whispering wind.
I hear the smiles around me,
how they dance out of my reach,
how they cackle without me,
but where it should hurt,
it feels...like nothing.
The only way I could feel it
is if I think of your voice
but I wont.
Because empty is exactly
the sound my deaf heart
can handle right now.

Better today

I am better today because
I honestly didn't have any further to fall
or anymore strength
to build anymore walls.
The night that I broke
and all hell slipped loose
after bruises, blood, and tears,
I begged me
for a truce.
I knew things were different
from that moment on.
There's no turning back
once the demons come out
and that's something I'm
very happy about.

Self-love

I love my sense of humor
it keeps me from getting hurt.
I love my mind
simply because of how busy it keeps me.
My body is excellent
at resisting pain
as it dances and runs
wildly all over the earth.
My sharp tongue
always lets people know
where I stand,
unapologetically, I continue to let it.
I love myself
for always finding a way
back into the light
even when the sun and stars
are gone.

That girl

That girl
she's out of her mind,
where she hides
I've yet to find.
She's such a mess
when she gets no sleep,
she's such a bitch
her words cut deep.
But when she loves
it's with all of her heart,
that girl,
has once, been
torn apart.

Backwards

She feels things backwards.
Pain welcomes her,
a warm and tight embrace
a constant flow of blood
the sound of a continuous heartbeat
that slowly slows
and the space she outgrows.
The tightness pushes her
back to the ground
and when she gets up
she realizes
she's found.

Mornings

I fell for you
as easy as the sun
enters the darkness at dawn,
and with every minute that passed
it got as strong as the sun shown brighter.
The mornings were ours
in a weird and magical way
but in the end
I knew you couldn't stay.
Sometimes I wonder
if it really even happened
or if it was just a dream,
and then the sun peeks
through the window
and my heart stings
just a little bit with love
and sadness.

Dreams

I love dreams that spill
into the next day.
The dreams that you visit
and all is right,
in the cozy, blanketed,
safety of my bed.
The dreams that I spend
actual time convincing
this heart of mine
that it was nothing more than
a ravishing trance
that I could die trying to
get back to, but must wait.
The dreams where
your voice is a calming breeze,
your laughter, a song.
The dreams where your heart
beats for the both of ours
because mine has stopped,
due to the beauty of such a mirage.
The dreams that remind me, that,
for a short time, you were mine.
And sometimes, on the right night, you still are.

I'm in charge

So perfect on the outside
so broken on the inside
I was your favorite heart to unlock.
Ripping me out of bed
rattled with shock,
jolting me alive at a dark 4 o'clock.
Forcing me to jump and move
on no sleep,
stability was never mine-
definitely not to keep.
Some days I own you now,
I've watched and waited
backing you into a corner,
now you have been baited.
When 4 o'clock rolls around
and I feel your cruel itch
I grab my running shoes,
hit the road,
and I make you my bitch.

Good morning depression,
I'm in charge today.

I hope

I hope
that one day,
when I find myself,
I will also find
forgiveness.

New

Some people
crack so deeply
that they can never heal.
They just have to
become a new person.

Tighter

I couldn't have held you any tighter
it was your time to leave.
I remind myself every day
that I will never see you again.
Just the thought of that seems silly.
You are my dad,
How can I not ever see you again?
But it's true. I won't.
And that fucks with me to no end.
I see children walking hand in hand
with their dads and I'm jealous.
I long for the simple warning
that in a flash, a heartbeat, a second
you would be gone.
I hold tight to your memory.
And sometimes I just hold myself
as tight as I can,
together.

Smile

I would like for people to stop asking me to smile.
This darkness that has now taken over, my body
doesn't care if you like me better that way.
I have never been able to fake a smile,
sadness sits itself deep into my eyes
my shoulders automatically slump
I look like I'm drifting through
but I feel like this tiny frame
weighs at least a ton.
It hurts to walk
but it hurts
more to
smile.

Awake

I'll never forget
the day the fog lifted.

I noticed things I hadn't seen in a lifetime,
like the light breeze that tickled my nose,
the trees and how they danced in the wind,
the birds singing me a welcome home song.
But what I noticed the most
is what it felt like,
from the inside out,
to enjoy this moment,
this day,
this life.

Suffering and acceptance

We weren't dressed for death
but when it came,
I only remembered
screaming your name.

Suffering and acceptance means more than
just acknowledging pain and that it is organic.
It requires reflection, so deep, that it is also subliminal.
Taking it apart. Laying it on the table. Analyzing
what fed into thoughts, ideas, and ultimately actions.
Pain doesn't just happen.
It grows over time. It is born and it overcomes you.
It takes your identityand rearranges your priorities.
It doesn't just start with looks, or glares, or words.
it thrives on silence.
It blossoms with blame and shame.
It is manifested with hostility and more silence. And then,
slowly, one unmet need at a time, its who you are.
Denial makes it unrecognizable in the mirror.
The only person
who can see it is the person who feeds it.
They manipulate you into thinking that it is a reality
that you created for yourself and its alarming to realize that,

over time, you had no control over this, because if you did-
you would've stopped it.
You would've called out the lies, the sulking, the mistrust, the
accusations, the belittling, the mocking, the excuses, the...
WHO THE HELL HAVE I BECOME?
One
Unmet
Need
At
A
Time.
At this point, it is just wise enough to know where it
started and how it was nourished.
And understand, the person who did this isn't bad.
He's just broken.
It is who he is now, too.
The only way to cut him off
is to kill the roots that live in you.

Bed

I am a slave to these blankets
they keep me wrapped and coddled,
tucked away from an unforgiving world.
My body is aching to move
but too tired to do so.
My mind is aching to live
but too anxious to do so.
I am surprised that I feel so safe
in this prison of sadness.
For if I am sleeping
I cannot do any harm.

Dreams

You have only visited my dreams twice,
Since you've died.
I call out to you
but my voice doesn't work.
I strain so hard to get your attention
but I cannot penetrate the barrier
of life and death in my dreams.
I wake up in a cold sweat
and I pray that you will
come back soon.

With you

There is no wrong way
with you.

We couldn't find a path
so we made our own.
Working against everybody
who says it can't be done.
We will catch so much hell
for the choices we make,
but as long as I'm beside you,
I don't care.
Our laughter will keep us afloat
in times of storms.
Our eyes will keep us connected
in times of silence.
Our love will keep us
wildly in awe of each other,
and nobody can take that away from us.
Soulmates.
As simple as that.

Chasing Myself

Goodbyes

Seduced by goodbyes,
I'm afraid it's no lie
that melancholy is all
that makes this heart fly.
With tears in these eyes
and no compromise
I long for the pain
of cloudier skies.

Lost

I look at all of the people
who I have been there for
and how they look at me now,
like I'm about to break.
Asking me how I'm doing
is just a way to tap dance
around an awkward "hello".
I say "I'm fine" as-fast-as-I-can.
But I don't blame them.
I'm just too sensitive now.
And they know that I will tell them
exactly what I think
and they won't like it.
The night that I fell apart,
I held nothing back
and lost everything.

Silence

And sometimes,
my favorite poem
is silence.

Night

I welcome the night
and the darkness
with open arms
and an insatiable laugh.
I'm not the least bit surprised
that the dark,
is scared of me.

Numb3rs

I
can't
buy milk
with the date
of your death on it.
I tell myself that they
are just numbers, but my
heart ~~doesn't~~ won't listen.

Away

The very last moments I ever spent with you were
you walking me down the aisle.
You were so proud that after years of conflict
and some with no contact had repaired themselves.
It was important that you and mom
forgive each other for the divorce.
You, symbolically gave me "away",
I felt so excited to step into a new life, but never wanted
to leave you behind after we became the best of friends.
Our Father/daughter dance,
I thought it was a joke that you chose "Sweet Caroline"
to dance to and was embarassed when I learned it wasn't.
You knew how much I hated that song, but it was
your favorite...just like me. So we danced and laughed.
I wish that my wedding wasn't the last time I saw you.
I am honored that you were there,
I am lucky that you were there,
I just didn't want to give you "away" yet.
Now heaven has you,
along with my heart.

Dreams

She dreams big,
for the past has bled her dry.
She dreams big,
for the tears
that have streamed
from hazel eyes.
She dreams big,
because she hasn't
dreamed in years.
She dreams big,
because she is
conquering her fears.

Tell her you're proud of her

She carries
the weight of the world
on her shoulders.
You'll find the strength in her eyes
to do so,
and the beauty
in her smile
to make it look easy.

Reflection

Today, I made it a point
to look deep
into her eyes.
I haven't in so long
and much to my surprise,
there were no tears.
Just somebody
who seems very strong.
This world hasn't been kind to her,
as anyone could see,
but that fighter,
looking back in the mirror...
that fighter is finally me.

Something

Something
in these old keys
makes me want to
just come apart.
An antiquated pain
that eerily calls
my heart it's home.
Was I born with it?
Do I attract it?
I'm finding more and more
that it is more a comfort
than a nuisance
and that terrifies me.
Something
in these old keys.

On earth...with me

I miss when
you walked
upon this earth,
but now that you
are a part of it,
I take less for granted.
Sunsets,
soft breezes,
and howling winds
remind me
that you are
still here,
on earth...with me.

Chasing Myself

Heal

I ran into the dead of the night
screaming for help,
but not the kind of help
you could give me.
I needed help from the devil himself.
I needed to feel the pain and anger
and rage that I had been hiding.
I needed to feel terror, sadness,
the burning of muscles,
a shortness of breath, and a rush of adrinaline.
After not feeling anything for so long,
I needed it all at once.
And with tears blinding my vision,
my hands and knees met the concrete
at the exact same time,
and I bled while I cried,
and I bled more than blood.
I bled my soul into a world of feeling
and decided it was time for healing.

Hearts heal

Hearts
eventually heal
harder,
stronger, and thicker.
Best of all,
they learn
to run quicker.

Laugh

Her silence
was often louder
than her voice,
but her laugh, touched everyone.
I've seen it wake entire
graveyards before,
bringing lonely souls home,
for their first time.

Chasing Myself

Beautiful

I'm not
beautiful
because
you said so.
I'm
beautiful
because
I'm
a fucking
survivor.

Some days I have
more than enough strength.
And those days
I feel beautiful
for all I have been through,
and who I came out as, in the end.
We should all celebrate
the beauty in surviving.

Dare

Some
days
I
dare
myself
to
move
on.
Today
I
accept
the
challenge.

-cwpoet

Thank you

Thank you, to all of you.

In one way or another, you've inspired me to open up about my history with depression, anxiety, and OCD. This book has been a tool for healing, for me, and hopefully you.

   Thank you Jeff, for your patience, space, and believing I was worth a second chance. Thank you Laura Frasier for helping me in more ways that any person should be equipt to do so. Thank you Laura Mills, for driving five hours to be here when I needed someone to help me stand.

Thank you, Suzan Hawkes for guiding me through all of these repressed emotions and laughing at them when I needed to.

Thank you Chandrea Pugh for living with me, over the phone, from so far away.

Thank you, to my brother, Peter, for always understanding me and helping me remember the good things about me.

Thank you, Susan Llewelyn, editor in chief and founder of ByMePoetry, for giving me the push I needed to continue my love affair with words.

Thank you, Keely and Eli, for making me want to be better, I couldn't be more blessed to have you as my children
-Mommy loves you!!!

Caroline

Made in the USA
Middletown, DE
07 February 2018